THE CHAOS OF ME

PATRICK S. SMITH

Contents

Preface

Thirty-five years. That is how long it took me to do this.

My journey into writing poetry started, like many people today, while in school. There they introduced me (a.k.a. forced to read) Shakespeare's sonnets, E. E. Cummings, Ralph Waldo Emerson, among others and forced to learn rhyme, schemes, and other mechanics of poetry. Everything that made poetry for me boring and uninteresting. This may be why, in part, I struggled with English and Literature.

That was until I read Edgar Allan Poe.

I was in the fourth or fifth grade when I first read any of Poe's poems. By this point I had read several of his short stories ("The Tell-Tale Heart", "The Cask of Amontillado", and "The Murders in the Rue Morgue" being chief among them) and found him enthralling. It was when I read and took part in a discussion on "The Bells," I saw a kind of magic in poetry. How the type of bell signified parts of our lives and how he used words to conjure up the sound of those bells. It proved to me all poetry didn't have to be "boring."

In the years that followed, I was mainly subjected to the same old poetry types that I didn't care for. However, occasionally, there were things like "Rime of Ancient Mariner," "Do not go gentle into that good night," and "To An Athlete, Dying Young" that excited me. Not for their "dark" content, but because they touched me. They awoke something deep within me I didn't have the words to describe then. Even more, the variety of styles showed me that I had been taught poetry all wrong.

Finally, came a pair of events that actually set me down this path.

The first, and I've told this story several times before, came during my Junior year in high school. I had a project where I had to either do a short story or ten poems. Initially, I had chosen to do a short story, but a computer crash and no back up forced me at the last minute to go the poetry route.

There was no attempt at any classic structure or rhyme scheme, just raw feelings and concepts. What some might call "words on a page," and I would have been glad to make a passing grade on it. Instead, I got my first 'A' in English.

The second was during Senior English, where I wrote a poem for class and to submit my High School journal. Being embittered at how the high school social system worked, I wrote the original "WhAT iS MaDNeSs," both as a pot shot back and to vent my frustrations. It felt good to get that out because, even today, I hate most of my experiences at that school.

Prior to my poem being submitted to the journal, my English teacher read it aloud for peer review. I think my teacher liked what I did, because he commented on some lines and the formatting. My classmates, on the other hand, said almost nothing. I don't know if they took it as a proverbial "punch in the face," missed the point of it, or something else. To the best of my knowledge, they didn't know I wrote it as the teacher never said who wrote what.

Sadly, it didn't get into the journal.

Since then, I've spun a few lines and verses, but never sought to get published. Mainly because I didn't know the process and never bothered to learn. Because of that, I lost many of those poems as I didn't think to keep them as well as I should have.

Which brings me to the chaos that is me.

A thirty-five-year glimpse of who I am, what I have gone through and what I've learned. The good, the bad, and the healing.

Contained here are some of the original ten poems, with some edits, that I wrote as a Junior thirty-five years ago and a new version of "WhAT iS MaDNeSs." Many of these poems are things I have written since high school, and each has a story behind it. Some dark, some humorous, and others reflective. But isn't that the chaos of life?

As I hinted before, I am not a fan of the classic structures and mechanics. This is not saying I don't use them (or at least attempt to use them), just that I don't mold my poetry into these forms. I let the poem dictate its form and sometimes it is close to one of these classic forms.

"Last Dance" and "Old Poems" are good examples of this as you could say they are "sonnet-ish" or "sonnet adjacent." They have some properties of a true sonnet, but not all. I'll let you, the reader, decide if they are truly sonnets or not.

If you enjoy these, don't worry. Though I prefer writing short stories, there are more of that original set I haven't published, and I get inspired to write more. This time, I won't wait thirty-five years to do this again.

Accomplishment and Attitude

The Mountain

I have conquered the mountain.
My Everest is now a mole hill.
But I dare not rest too long,
For I see another mole hill,
In the guise of Everest,
Waiting to be conquered.

Success

What is success?
Fame and fortune?
Maybe something simpler -
All in the eye of the beholder.

You may think me a failure.
I disagree.
I have tried,
So I have not failed.

Success I have not found,
You may argue.
I have,
I will counter.

You are now my proof.
You found my pages,
You see the words I wrote.
And for a moment,
I have entered your mind.
That is my success.

I will admit,
I hunger for more.
I will never be a true bard,
But you talking about me,
Makes me more successful,
Than I dared to dream.

The Monkeys on My Back

Once upon my back,
There sat a monkey,
It hung like a sack,
Always restraining me.

In time that past,
On me it did pull,
I thought I could not last,
And I felt like a fool.

Then, as I completed my task,
The monkey left my back.
And entered two gorillas.

Named Confidence and Patience,
They wore pin-striped suits,
And sat upon the sofa.

The monkeys then fled,
I did not know there were two,
And they cowered from the gorillas.

When they were on my back,
They weighed me down,
Trying to deny me my goal.

Doubt and Fear they were,
Restraints to withhold me,
Attempting to usurp my dreams.

When I achieved my mark,
They lost their hold on me,
And looked to regain.

To me the gorilla's explained,
Doubt and Fear's purpose:
They were to dissuade me,
Not allow me to succeed,

When I was done,
And proof in my hand,
The gorillas introduced themselves.

The first was Confidence,
The knowledge that I can,
And the other Patience,
The power to see it through.

Now they serve to inspire,
Remind me of what I have done,
And to guard against monkeys.

Why I Write

I think.
I feel.
I imagine.
I dream.
Therefore,
I write

The Path

I sense the path before me.
Eyes closed, I begin to sprint.
Not a step is taken,
Before I stumble and fall.

I get up and run again,
Only to fall once more.
Laying dejected I wonder,
Why can I not run?

I open my eyes,
To see before me.
The path is full of obstacles,
It cannot be traversed.

Once more I attempt to run.
Falling repeatedly.
I look to myself,
To see my legs are too weak,

So I start to crawl.

Navigating the obstructions.

Strength and confidence build.

As I clear each one.

Now I attempt to walk,
The first steps are unsure.

I trip and stumble often,
Until my footing is secure.

Soon I am running.
Not the sprint of before,
A measured comfortable pace,
So I can navigate the path.

When I pause to reflect,
As the path continues on.
I see the miles I have come,
The obstacles that lay behind me.
My spirit is renewed,
As I resume my run down the path.

Anthology

A thousand stories to tell,
A thousand poems to recite,
A thousand songs to sing,
A thousand pictures to paint.

The kaleidoscope of imagination,
The chaos of visions,
The whispers of inspiration,
Run wild in fertile minds,

Brush, chisel, pen and hand,
All the tools of man,
To push back the darkness.

Each an unyielding candle,
A never ending light,
Casting dreams to others.

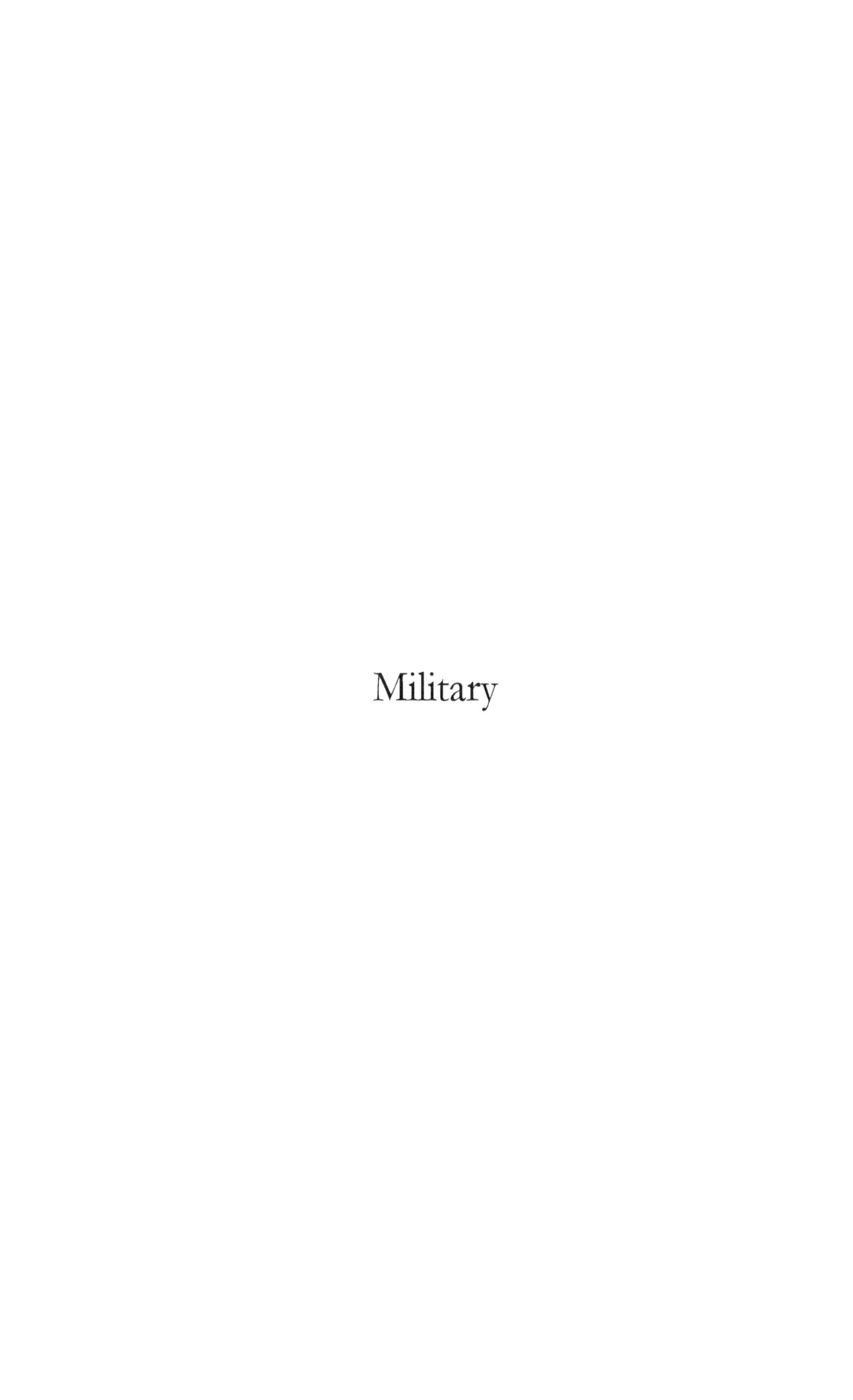

Military

Mail Call

Messages from home,
Brief electric flashes.
A quick few lines,
From dear old friends,
Beaming with well wishes,
And "come home soon."

Words conjuring memories,
Of days nearly forgotten.
Painting a vision,
About another world.
So very long ago,
And so very far away.

Serving as anchor,
Holding my brothers and I,
The strangers in a strange land.
Tying us back to home,
Reminding us who we are;
Where we came from.

Photos from home,
Weathered post cards.
Snapshots of parents,
With time worn faces.
Pictures of children,
Babies with fathers unseen.

News of an exotic land,
At times seeming so foreign.
Places and people,
I long so much to see,
Breathe in again,
Or simply just hold.

Simple things to be missed,
Treasured times never had.
Grandparent's smiles of love,
A child's first steps,
All day tea parties,
That I would try to avoid.

Letters from home,
Simple scraps of paper;
Tattered and worn.
Hand written script,
Teasing with odors,
From a lost time.

Another mail call,
Creating giddy excitement,
Like kids at Christmas,
Eye wide with hope and awe.
But tainted with a fear,
Of a letter for "John."

A priceless treasure,
Kept close at heart.
Bringing night filled dreams,
Of being home with you,
Only to wake to the nightmare,
That I'm not there.

Letters from home,
A collection of priceless treasures,
Hope of better days,
As they tear at my heart.
Lending strength to handle all woes,
Giving meaning to a chaotic world.

HEROES

Children sometimes ask,
"What is a hero?"
Is it something from a comic,
Or a character in a movie?
Are they larger than life?
Bound to do great things?

I have learned what a HERO is,
A heavy cost to know this,
Paid on that fateful day,
A lesson never forgotten,
Burned into my memory,
Like a painting in a museum.

On that terrible morning,
Chaos and Hell reigned.
Death from the sky,
The innocent the intended victim.
The aim was true,
And by scores they fell.

Through the chaos,
HEROES emerged,
Charging like knights of old,
After demons and dragons.
Their cause simple and noble:
To help those in need.

Boldly striding into the inferno,
Past the gates of Hell,
Into the abode of the Devil.
They each did more,
Than any human should,
Or ever thought possible.

Tirelessly they fought,
Knowing so much rode on them,
That countless others needed them.
Each took their turn,
To stare Death in the face,
Until Death itself flinched.

But at last, unlike the knights,
Death and Time finally won.
The damage to great to hold,
Two mountains of steel fell,
Burying alive the HEROES,
Still trying to save others.

While these HEROES fought,
Another group of HEROES,
Heard tales of the tragedy.
And so, they began their own fight,
To protect the innocent unknown.
To Earth they fell, in an empty field.

The HEROES' names, I do not know,
Save one – Father Mike, all are revered.
For a bard once wrote:
"The brave experience death only once"
To that I would add:
And a HEROES spirit is immortal.

Since then, I have been called a hero,
Because some think I have acted as one,
And I shun that distinction,
I feel I'm not worthy,
To stand the shadow of a HERO,
Though I strive to be like them.

The Day I Became a New Yorker

I was Southern born, Southern bred.
Of all that is Yankee,
I had no use.
Little good came from the North.

Twice I had ventured north,
Twice when I came back south,
My boots burned,
For touching tainted soil.

September 11, 2001,
Watching the horror as it unfolded.
Some things inside of died.
My pride, arrogance, and innocence.

Two suicide planes,
Aimed at our hearts and souls,
They missed their mark,
And struck the Towers instead.

I felt my rage grow,
Why would someone do this?
How could someone do this?
My blood began to stir.

I had no family or friends,
Martyred in some evil's cause.
Three thousand souls,
Name one, I did not know.

Still, I felt the pain.
Lives torn asunder
Questions unanswered.
Disbelief that this was happening.

Later, I heard of brave souls,
Who fought to the biter end,
Trying to protect those trapped,
Stuck in Hell's inferno.

I longed to do something,
To try to help those suffering.
I would get my chance,
But that is a later date.

Slowly I realized,
My pride misplaced
Yes, I am Southern,
But I'm an AMERICAN FIRST.

That simple thing,
Bonded me to all Northerners,
Like sworn blood brothers
It rallied me to try to be their pillar.

Nothing I could do directly to help,
But my call finally came,
Not a call for vengeance,
But a much sweeter drink – Justice.

My innocence stripped from me,
Like the husk from corn.
I vowed that very day,
No one would suffer like that again.

I now yearn to go north again.
To walk that hallowed ground
Where the Towers fell,
I revere it the same as Pearl Harbor

For on September 11, 2001,
Much to a younger me's chagrin,
I became what I disliked the most,
I became a New Yorker.

Launch

I launch this plane,
Its mission I do not know,
As it departs,
I offer simple hopes:

If you are flying to train,
Then may those you train,
    Make the best look second rate.

If you are to face the enemy,
Then may they seek Hell,
    As a refuge from your wrath.

If you are to provide comfort,
Then may the Angle of Mercy,
    Learn compassion from you.

And if you are to bring troops home,
Then may the Breath of God clear your way,
    And His hands lift your wings.

Family and Love

"Daughter"

Though not of my blood,
From the first I claimed you.
As I said unto your mother,
"Till death do us part,"
So to you I echoed,
Those same words.

At times chasms made,
Paths have been rough.
But you have always been part of my purpose.
No challenge was too great.
For you to seize the world,
Is my dream for you.

Finally, you came to me.
As a woman in a final acceptance,
With a single question,
That I said "yes" to:
"Dad, will you adopt me?"
A day I shall always cherish, my daughter.

So know this my child,
We have built bridges and cleared roads,
And words I gave your mother,
I now reaffirm to you my daughter,
"For better or worse,"
"Till death do us part."

A Child Should Not Mourn

A child should not mourn,
No tears of loss,
Light darkened by sadness,
Nor gloom allowed to prevail.

For it is their duty,
To replace all grief with joy,
Wipe away all darkness,
And light the world anew.

The Broken Time

It is 5:05,
The clock is broken,
Time comes to a crawl,
As I sit and wait.

In another room,
My loved one stays,
They are hurt - stressed,
Here I sit and wait.

The minutes pass,
Impatience filling me,
To hear a word,
And I sit and wait.

I bounce my feet,
On a page,
Words I see,
And I sit and wait.

Now at 5:06,
My coffee is gone,
A new cup I get,
To resume, sit and wait.

I glance to the TV,
Words I do not hear,
The picture stays still,
As I sit and wait.

I stand and pace,
Around the room,
Walk I do,
Better than to sit and wait.

After an hour,
I turn to the clock,
To see it is 5:08,
I must sit and wait.

A door opens,
I look to see,
But it is not for me,
Again, I sit and wait.

I close my eyes,
To nap may restore time,
And bring news,
As I sit and wait.

When I awake,
The clock shows 5:11,
And I resolve,
To sit and wait.

Finally word comes,
My loved one is fine,
Upon the clock I look,
Time is restored,
It is 8:54,
I close my eyes in relief,
A moment later I see them,
And my restlessness is gone,
Soon we will go home,
So I sit and wait.

Last Dance
(Sonnet 1)

Give me one last dance,
And let me wish it would last.

Let me have one more kiss,
'Cause it, I will always miss.

Give me a final embrace,
For I know, lost is this race.

For when the music ends,
Only memories will remain.
And all that was, can never be.
A new chapter must begin,

Let it be a song full of new hopes
A new dance with new partners,
And new dreams to be forged
So please, one last dance.

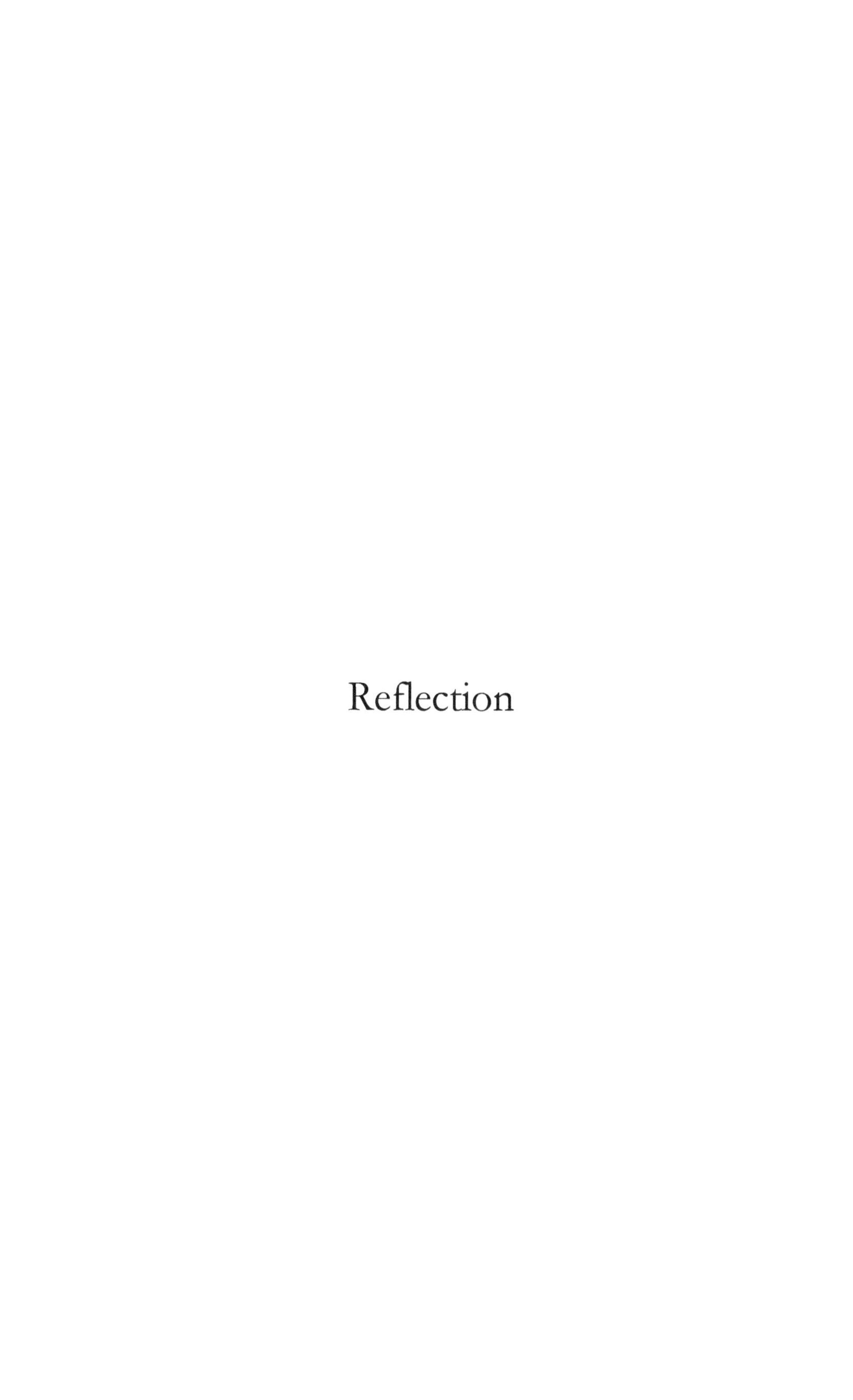

Reflection

Lost Poems

A feeling,
A line,
A verse.
Like a vapor,
Caught in the wind,
It is now gone.

A feeling,
A line,
A verse.
Pen to paper,
Caught in time,
But the paper is now gone.

How many verses,
How much of my work,
How much of my soul,
Is forever gone?

Colors

I sit down to create,
An infinite pallet before me.
Where to start,
Which to choose.

The first is too muted,
The next to subtle,
I discard so many,
They just won't do.

In the end,
A handful remain.
Each a sharp contrast to the others.
The few is better.

To paint my soul,
Too much would blur that,
And cloud the image.
Let others see my extremes,
And infer the subtitles,
In the few colors that remain.

My Wasted Youth

My wasted youth,
Of days gone by,
Things not done,
Words not said.

Ambitions that passed,
Like clouds in sky,
Goals not met,
Dreams all but dead.

Tomorrow is uncertain,
But I have this moment,
Seize it I will,
Regret will no longer burden,
No more postponements,
These aspirations I must fulfill.

Where Do My Loyalties Lay?

Where do my loyalties lay?
Not here,
For I sense no trust.

From where I came?
I do not know,
For my comrades are slipping away.

To myself?
Yes, but they are not there,
Because I cheat myself of self's own glory.

To my country?
To a degree,
Because that Dream has begun to fade.

One day,
Chance permitting,
I will discover where my loyalties lay.

Two Dark Paths

I.

Two dark paths,
Before me I see.
One shadowed and chill,
Second black and still.

Two dark paths,
Which one for me?
Both are forbidding,
Neither is inviting.

Two dark paths,
How shall it be?
One shadowed and chill,
A rocky bitter trail,
False dreams and hollow joys,
Nothing to be treasured,
Only pain and suffering.

Two dark paths,
What will be?
Second black and still,
Empty,
Grief,
Void,
Final.

Two dark paths,
Before me I see.
One shadowed and chill,
Second black and still.

II.

Two dark paths,
How foolish of me!
So many had come before,
With illuminating wisdom,
Trying to show other trails,
That I refused to heed.

Two dark paths,
What I could see,
Now I know the folly,
Of my younger self,

Two dark paths,
Not meant to be.
Those two paths as I saw,
I thought bight and happy,
Were all the world.
Alas, how little I really knew.

Two dark paths,
Always before me.
Meant only turmoil or ruin,
No salvation or hope.

Two dark paths,
Now that I can see,
Infinite other brighter paths,
Have always been there.
Never clear, never easy,
But always there.

Two dark paths,
I will let be,
My riches and reward,
They lay down different trails.

Two dark paths,
That I never wish to see.
New travelers come this way,
Some deaf and blind,
Heedless of the consequences,
Down the two dark paths they go.

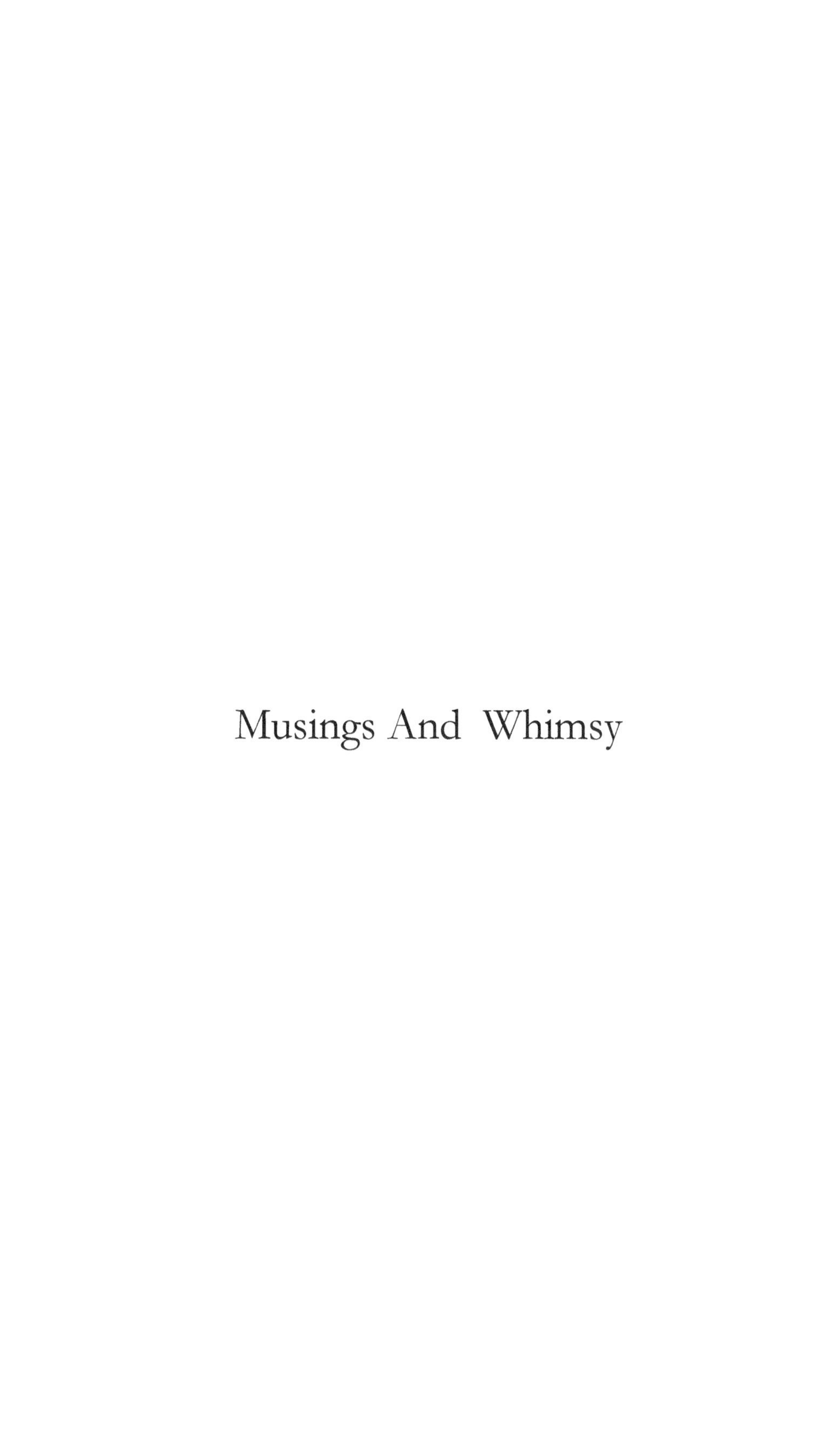

Musings And Whimsy

Why Is It So

Why is it so?
That we, such lovers of peace,
Make ways of destroying one another,
When we could be saving some other.

Why is it so?
We destroy in moments,
What took sweat to build.
Why can't we save another?

Why is it so?
Our babies must kill one another,
When a Madman says to,
When they could be playing together.

Why is it so?
That our War technology,
Far exceeds our PEACE knowledge?
That we fight over our differences,
When understanding joins us.
Please, tell me,
Why is it so?

Technology

Our lives are affected by it,
It has come to be our friend,
    Our ally, our enemy.
It tells us when we error and when were right.

It helps us to live,
To let us survive,
It helps to make us die.

We have come to depend on it,
But when we most need it,
The blasted technology always fails us.

Old Poems
(Sonnet 2)

I stop and wonder,
What happens to a poem,
After is read,
And it then becomes old?

Does its tome,
Become its tomb?
The words and verses,
To fade to the ether.

Or is it like a seed?
Hidden, laying dormant,
Until at last it sees,
A new spring sun,
Awaken what is inside,
And it can blossom again.

The Blade

I am presented a blade,
Careful I must be,
As it is wicked sharp,
Beyond all imaginations.

Carefully I take it,
And use it to refine my work,
Cleanse the strong,
Cutting out the weak.

I present the blade to another,
To do the same as I have done,
Careful I must be.
The blade cuts two ways.
Giver and taker must know this,
Lest be cut by the blade.

Sleep Eludes Me

Sleep eludes me as the dream remains,
Hours pass and I cannot rest,
The darkness of night around me.

In this weary and bleary state,
My muse comes unto my mind,
There to dance and whisper to me.

I am given visions and thoughts,
Though I yearn to sleep,
But she will not let it be.

These things I am given,
Each a treasure unto its own,
I wish to be at a different hour,
All is lost if I dare tarry.

Her call and song I give attention,
Begrudgingly I do rise,
To light and to pen and to paper,
To craft her cage before she departs.

The New Year

A new year has begun,
What changes does it hold?
What alteration should I make?
What goals to be met?

Through the years gone past,
The machine really hasn't changed,
New assemblies to replace old,
But it still runs the same.

On occasion, a gear does break,
Or a part does fail.
Adjustments are made,
But it still runs the same.

I try to better,
By my own view,
And those around me,
But it still runs the same.

We live,
We love,
We pass on,
And the year runs the same.

The Snow Fall

White cotton from the sky,
Lazily it drifts on the wind,
Ode to cherry blossoms petals,
That will fly in the spring.

The dance, the swirl,
The pirouette as they fall,
Each to its own time,
Displaying their own beauty.

Some may curse or swear,
At the inconvenience,
Roadways to be cleared,
Walks to be shoveled.

For the moment I will sit,
Amaze at the choreography,
Of this ethereal wonder,
And revel in the majesty.

Bedtime Routine

I make my final rounds,
The doors are secure,
Dread fills me as I lay down,
For now I realize,
This day has ended in 'y,'
So tomorrow is Monday.

The Chaos of Me

WhAT iS MaDNeSs

A.

Why do you say I am mad?
    Just because I see things you do not.
 The world I perceive,
  Is far different than yours.
Catch sight thru my eyes,
Demons and witches are about.

  The world is different to me,
Unique to all as it should be.

Boxes that hold small things,
    Guarded by so many hobgoblins.
  And I fear them not.
 A cacophony of drummers,
    Guide my steps.

Do not pad me in,
    For not viewing things as you.
  My mind is my own,
  Free to think and to wonder.
Nor cast me out in ostracism,
    When I tell you my truth.
There are those like me,
Who question the world.

Cast off the shackles,
That tie your wits to the ground,
Then you begin to understand,
That I am not a drone or mad.

II.

I am completely sane,
My mind conforms to the normal.
I see the world how it is,
And how it should be for all.

I read a bookE,
It shows me how to think,
There are others who say the same,
And I add my voice to the chorus.

Eat,
Sleep,
Think,
As the others.

Eat,
Sleep,
Think,
As the others.

Eat,
Sleep,
Think,
As the others.

Those who dare to question,
Or not follow the bookE,
They need to be helped,
Lest they be shunned.

To think outside the norm,
That is insanity.
To join and conform,
Is the path away from madness.

What Stares Back From the Mirror?

What stares back from the mirror?
Simple reflections, tricks of light,
A view of outer myself,
As I appear to the world

Meer glass and metal,
Shaped and worked.
Made by Man's hand,
To work its unnatural magic.

What stares back from the mirror?
The creature inside,
Struggling for control,
Fighting to get out.

Abrogation, monstrous visage,
A blighted sore to the eye.
Right and decent character,
Making the world a better place.

What stares back from the mirror?
An angel within,
Trapped in a cage
Scrambling to be free.

Beauty and graceful views,
An elegant vision to behold.
Shallow and callous nature,
Tearing at other's souls.

What stares back from the mirror?
All my failures and short comings.
All that I could have ever been,
But I never achieved to be.

This vision I do not like,
But it is always there staring back.
Making it oh so easy,
To turn away in despair.

What stares back from the mirror?
Infinite dreams and desires.
Everything that I should ever be
If only I were to make it so.

An inspiring view it is,
Always waiting to lift me up.
Daring me to reach higher,
No matter the chains trying to hold me down.

What exactly is it?
That which stares back from the mirror?

The Noir and the Dark

There exists in my mind,
Many places and chambers,
Some bright and inviting,
Other, not so much.

With the bright places,
Though they are boring,
I keep these displayed,
Welcome all who wish to see.

The Noir and the Dark,
The recesses I onced dwelled,
Some now, I wish to reside,
Others, I just acknowledge.

These are old haunts,
Some have I just re-found,
Others I've known all along,
The Noir and the Dark.

Shattered dreams of old,
Things that could have been,
Adorn the very walls,
As a haunted memory.

My demons of old,
Now long vanquished,
Others still walk beside me.
In the Noir and the Dark.

Elsewhere there exists,
A plethora of treasure,
Words, verses and tomes,
Things not yet shared.

Some which I thought lost,
Others I did not know exist,
Layers of dust obscures it all,
Hiding it from the light.

Here I choose to linger,
Polishing what I have found,
To share this is my desire,
From the Noir and the Dark.

The Chaos of Me

The Chaos of Me,
You wish to see?
Then these rules,
You must obey.

Your arms and hands,
Keep to yourself,
Don't look at the animals,
As they are not there,
They are part of,
The Chaos of Me.

A thousand tears shed,
This Chaos of Me,
Hidden behind,
A thousand laughs.

The noise you hear,
Is the soundtrack of,
The Chaos of Me,
A thousand musicians,
Out of tune,
Out of time,
Playing different songs.

The Chaos of Me,
Countless highs I have endured,
And celebrated as many lows.

In my eyes I see,
A kaleidoscope of color,
All in black in white,
And all the grays,
In the Chaos of Me,
Are an infinite spectrum,
Of colors unimagined.

The calm you perceive,
Is my tempest of emotions,
Ever fueled by,
The Chaos of Me.

Every mask I have worn,
In the Chaos of Me,
Is both the lie,
And the truth,
Of what I am.

And since you have glimpsed,
A small sampling of,
The Chaos of Me,
Do you now dare acknowledge,
The Chaos of You?

If you enjoyed this, please be sure to leave a comment and follow me at patrickssmithauthor.wordpress.com. You can also check out my other works.

Other books by Patrick S. Smith

Tales of the Seeress

My Time Among the Elves (Coming soon)

About the Author

Patrick S. Smith lives in Columbus, Georgia with his wife and daughters. He is a 20-year veteran of the U.S. Air Force Reserves. He enjoys knitting, playing video games, and watching a variety of sports.
He has been writing off and on for thirty-five years. Now he is using his imagination to bring forth his wonderful new world and people.